Let Go, Embrace Change and Have Fun!

Living the Joyful Life You Design

Karen Jones

Copyright © KScope Focus, 2018
All Rights Reserved

ISBN 978-1790171170
Library of Congress Control Number 2017942902
Book Cover designed by: Akivda M

Without limiting the rights under copyright reserved above, no part of this publication may be reproduced, stored in or introduced into a retrieval system, or transmitted, in any form or by any means (electronic, mechanical, photocopying, recording, or otherwise), without the prior written permission of both the copyright owner and the above publisher of this book.

The scanning, uploading, and distribution of this book via the internet or via any other means without the permission of the publisher is illegal and punishable by law. Please purchase only authorized electronic editions and do not participate in or encourage electronic piracy of copyrighted materials. your support of the author's rights is appreciated.

Dedication:

To Johanna Austin, who lived a full 100 years.

To Leonora and John Grunfelder, who provided the start to my journey and taught me how to embrace change,

and

To Amy McGinness, who carries my legacy to have fun with the next generation.

Testimonials

"If you are stuck, hit a wall, and don't know how you are ever going to do it or are struggling to figure it out, this book is exactly what you need."

Karen Mayo, CEO, Author, Mindful Eating, TEDx Speaker
"Mindful Eating with Mayo"

"This book is a great resource. I've learned in my own journey that it's an inside job. It's like an onion, peeling back layer by layer to find resolution and peace.

If you want practical, specific and challenging guidance and an exercise to help you achieve what you want to do, this is the right book! Go at your own speed, find your own way!"

Pattie DeNunzio, Account Executive, North American Title Company

"Karen Jones has shown us some of the lessons she has learned and pointed to areas we can consider in developing our own path. This is a good starting point. For those further down their own path, it is a reminder of where you have come from and areas you may have taken a side turn and want to refine your direction."

Ilene Strong, MSgt, USAF (Retired)

"Just Let Go, Embrace Change and Have Fun delivers a wealth of information in an easy read for anyone facing the challenges of wanting to make a change in their life. Karen understands how resistance due to feelings of overwhelm can derail you from the life you desire."

Jane Deuber, CEO, Global Experts Accelerator

"Just Let Go, Embrace Change and Have Fun is a small book with a big kick for self-empowerment and fun. In a very comprehensive, clear, concise and easy to understand manner Karen addresses the components of all areas of life; physical, mental, emotional and spiritual. And, the exercises are easy to follow. Doing them you'll not only learn to overcome obstacles but move beyond and have fun and enjoy life. I recommend this book to anyone who has these goals in life."

Penny Cohen, LCSW Transformational Psychotherapy Author of Personal Kabbalah: 32 Paths to Inner Peace and Life Purpose and her new work in Progress: Transform Your Life in 21 Minutes: Freeing One Obstacle at a Time©

"I am a big fan and believer in the principles taught by Karen Jones in her book. Very insightful, easy to read and potentially life-changing for the person who truly wants more out of life."

Mark Larson, President, Larson & Company Real Estate

"If you're ready to embrace big change, make a smart pivot, and get going on your most important plans, goals, and dreams - grab Karen's book, read it, mark it up, listen to her wise advice and you WILL make it happen."

David Newman, Author of Do It! Marketing

You can sit back and watch, or hop on for the adventurous ride of your life! There's no guarantee how much time we have, so let's get moving and have fun.

~Karen Jones

Introduction

Everyone has the same starting place and ending place. What happens in the middle is your choice!

You have a path to follow just as I do. The only difference is you choose which path to follow. Just like the plane flying overhead, you see its path across the sky. You too have a path.

You can either follow what you see left by someone else or pave your own way. The path the plane travels across the blue sky is clear and distinct. With time, the path fades. Similarly, you can follow a clear path or wait, and push through the blurred path, or figure it out on your own.

This book is about the journey to connect with the most important person in your life. We have many distractions on our journey. When you focus on what provides clarity for you, you will find the path you were meant to follow.

Life is an adventure. It was a long time before I realized I love to go exploring.

This book is about the adventure to the life you desire. There is no accelerator or brake on this adventure. You will know which adventure is right for you. My purpose is to provide the guide to imagine what's possible.

When you connect with who you are and find your path, the person inside emerges and you will feel proud, courageous and joyful.

This book is a journey to explore your adventure, curiosity, and creativity.

The topics are provided to guide your deeper self-discovery. Each section has an action to take, or quiz to complete on your journey. The real-time exploration is up to you.

Whether you decide this is a virtual test or reality, when you are ready to explore more deeply, you can revisit each chapter for deeper adventure.

This is not a one trip journey. You can repeat your journey with more depth and truth the next time.

This is personal, with no judgments. If you feel you cannot make a decision because you want support, I am here for you. You are the only one that can tell if this is the right step.

When it does not feel right, honor yourself that you learned something by your decision. It was right at this moment. With your experience, you will know there is another option available for you.

Feel free to record your thoughts and feelings as you experience each chapter.

I have added journal pages at the end of each section for your comments. If you prefer use a composition book to make your accompanying comments. Write in pen, and add the date to your entry, so you can review your journey and revisit your journal to see your progress.

Your comments support your decision making and the steps you have taken. The journal will also help you validate your progress toward the life you desire.

This is your time to accept who you are and where you are without comparison to anyone else.

This is your time, your journey!

Table of Contents

What Does Your Stuff Represent? 12
    Physical Stuff 13
    Mental Stuff 14
    Our Choices Impact Everything We Do 17
    Spiritual 18
    Stuff You Lose 20
    Celebrity Stuff 21
    Still Waiting For An Update 22
    The Update 23
Do You Have Obstacles, Walls And Boundaries? 27
    Obstacles 29
    Walls 32
    Boundaries 33
    Breaking Through 34
What Fuels You 39
    Nutrition 40
    Brain Food 42
    Food Cooperatives 43
    Inflammation 45
    Water 48
Do You Have The Energy 55
    Move Your Body 56
What Is Your Sleep 'N Beauty Routine? 66
    Food 70
    Caffeine 71
    Light or Noise Pollution 71
    TV 72
    Cell Phone and Social Media 73
    Alarm Clock or Not 74
    Room Temperature 74
    Sleep Routine 74
    Fresh Air / Exercise 75

Sleep Aids 75
Do You Have Hobbies and Schedule Fun? 79
    Next Phase 84
    Hobbies are FUN! 87
    Do you Schedule FUN? 88
What About Your Spirituality Practice? 91
    Here Is The Drama 93
    Here Is How To Calm The Drama With A Time Out 95
    Stress Is The Mindful Chatter 96
    Take An Outdoor Break 97
    Meditation Is Your Inner Experience 97
    Vision Or Mantra 98
    Clarity And Focus 100
Are You Satisfied With Your Relationships? 103
    Communication 107
    Socializing 109
    Breaking the Ice 110
    Communication Tips 111
Have You Arrived At Joy? 113
    Adventure 115
    Positivity 116
    Love 117
    Gratitude 117
    Thank You 118
About the Author 119
Her website is www.kscopefocus.com 120
Gratitude for Support on My Journey 121

What Does Your Stuff Represent?

Some people would say "stuff" represents their worldly possessions while others call it clutter, and yet others call it your drama. It is all the above. Your stuff is all about you.

We all have different attachments. Your physical, mental and spiritual stuff is all about you. Let's define each one and how important they are in your life.

Physical Stuff

Physical stuff are the objects that surround you. The objects in your kitchen, living room, bedroom, clothes, your car, jewelry and everywhere else.

Remember when you were moving out of your parent's house? There were things you knew you needed to set up your own household. Your parents, or grandparents may have given you items they no longer needed to help you. Additionally, there were trips to the local thrift shop, or visits to local yard sales for your own household "goodies."

My first apartment was an eclectic collection of all the above. Today, I have let go of most of the items. I have kept only a few items I cannot live without.

Whether it is a picture that hangs in my hallway, a mirror that reminds me of a visit to Cape Cod, or a picture I picked up at a craft fair that I could not live without. We all have those items that make our home, uniquely ours and equally feel it is a part of us.

There are times when we accumulate more stuff than we physically can use or "need." It is about the 15th pair of heels to wear with your black cocktail dress for a special occasion, or the collection of sweats we choose when our body expands when we are not feeling our best.

It is also the collection of whatever goods we *must* buy to satisfy a void in our life rather than face a reality and begin the change process.

Everyone has a time when they must face the reality to make a change. If you feel you would like help, there are professional organizers to help you choose what you use and what can be disposed. The disposal process can be donating to local thrift shops, and taking tax deductions.

Mental Stuff

The Mental stuff you are attached to is very different.

~~~~~~~~~

It is the feelings, thoughts and experiences that fill your mind with stress, negative self-talk, sadness and require more energy to manage.

~~~~~~~~~

There are situations in life when we are consumed with what does not serve us. When you are in an unhappy or dark place and nothing seems to alleviate your pain, it is time to seek professional help.

I also pursued professional support to release the negative self-talk and sadness I felt about myself.

What Does Your Stuff Represent?

For six years, I suffered with post-partum depression before I realized what it was. I was continually getting sick. My immune system was depleted. I was not sleeping well and I could not understand how having a healthy baby could cause me such mental and emotional pain.

I had all the signs of a happy life from the outside, but I was not happy. I had a job I enjoyed. The success in my career always provided another challenge. I was promoted several times, and each time with more responsibility, and subsequently increased pay. I also faced the struggle of balancing my own stress and balance in my life for all my responsibilities. I had a great husband and the house of my dreams.

Yet, I found it difficult to get out of bed each morning because I felt depleted of energy before the day started. I also was not sleeping well. I thought maybe marriage counselling would help because it seemed that other areas of my life were affected by my pain.

Finally, I decided to get personal counselling. My own dark tunnel was causing me to reflect and admit I needed help.

I felt better through therapy and felt relief from my depression. You may not know you need help until you start talking to others to discover they have also travelled a similar journey.

There are options available for professional mental help whether you can afford the services or not. I would recommend checking for local community services or a mental health professional. There are various counselling options available with varying pricing options.

The personal investment is worthwhile and the benefits last a lifetime.

~~~~~~~~

 *Because of seeking professional help, I found there was more internal self-talk to work on that I originally thought.*

~~~~~~~~

I came to terms with my overbearing father during my teenage years. I identified I needed to resolve these challenges. I was the only one who could change how I felt.

I had to address the feelings that surfaced in my teenage years with my lack of privileges and trust. My father was doing his parental duty to protect me.

I felt a constant heavy hand and loud voice to keep me "in control" and restricted me from being the carefree teenager I wanted to be.

Many times, as a teenager, I dreamed of running away and concluded "Where would I go?" This ongoing struggle as a teenager impacted my self-esteem.

Our Choices Impact Everything We Do

I made choices when I started college and I did not finish for financial reasons. These decisions haunted me for more than ten years and affected my self-confidence in my career. Despite my facade to be conversational, professional and outgoing, I was giving the impression of being "in control," and internally, I felt like an imposter.

I discovered it was easier not to speak up. For many years, I paid the price by being quiet and refrained from sharing my feelings. My voice became inaudible in my head.

During my adolescence, I learned it was "best" to keep quiet, keep my thoughts to myself. I continued the same behavior in my professional career.

For more than 20 years I did not speak up. I learned that holding in my feelings and opinions was not healthy. I had been quiet and did not express my feelings, which later surfaced as hostility and anger.

The lesson cost me many relationships. Every day I am learning, while it is challenging to speak up, it is necessary to express how I feel. When I do, I can feel the tension released in my body.

Holding on to the mental clutter is not healthy.

The sooner you can release it, the healthier you will feel. It took me a long time to realize this.

I did not always choose the best time to release my frustration and anger.

My lesson learned was when you carry the physical and mental clutter, your body becomes rigid, and movements are restrictive. Relaxing is more challenging with each year passing. When this restriction is continued for years, it shows up in stress, and disease you must address proactively.

Stress and anger are stored in the body. They rob you of freedom of movement and joy in your life.

Spiritual

Spiritual attachments are different to everyone. Spiritual attachments can refer to your religion. When you do have a formal religion, it provides a path. It can also be the path you follow to enable you the flexibility to live through situations in your life.

~~~~~~~~

I view my spiritual stuff as the virtues that provide daily guidance. The virtues of faith, hope, love, patience, kindness, forgiveness, grace, charity and integrity.

~~~~~~~~

It may be the daily practice you follow which differs from the familial religious practices you grew up with. The new beliefs you practice may be those you acquired since living on your own.

Spiritual stuff represents the behaviors you practice to replenish when you feel stifled. When life events go well, you forget about spiritual support. In contrast, when you need guidance, you know where to reach out to those who can support and replenish when you feel depleted.

Here's A Recent Insight About My Stuff

How would you feel if you lost all your "stuff?" I am sitting in my new apartment with two boxes of clothes, a box of my financial and legal files, a box of my training materials and books for my business, my laptop, printer and two-fold up camping chairs waiting for my worldly possessions to arrive.

The POD (the latest, most convenient and economical mobile container for moving) company's customer service representative said it would arrive today!

Some would feel relief if they could file a claim and get new stuff to start over (with less and you do not have to unpack).

Others feel it is impossible to recapture all their stuff that is lost. Possessions are stuff! Do you have emotional attachment to your stuff?

Most days I feel it would be a relief to live with much less. I have downsized over the past ten years from a four-bedroom house to a one-bedroom cottage.

In that time, I have moved four times and every time, procrastinated getting rid of stuff. Slowly I have donated to the local Thrift Shop or carted off boxes to Goodwill what I no longer use and want to help others.

I have moved beyond the garage sale days as I feel my time is more valuable than sitting for a day or two waiting for lookers to check for their next treasure.

Two of my moves were only eight miles away and caused me the most significant downsizing from married life to single person lifestyle. Each move has prompted my decisions of what is important about moving to the next location and what I can truly let go.

Stuff You Lose

Vividly, I remember seeing the news footage of Hurricane Katrina about the residents that lost everything. They were victims who did not have the luxury of deciding to let go of anything.

They lost everything. The same holds true for Hurricane Hermine in the fall of 2016. Everyone loves their stuff. When catastrophe strikes, the true test of what is important is expressing gratitude that God saved you and your family, and yes, your stuff can be replaced.

Celebrity Stuff

Over five years ago, Barbra Streisand went through a de-cluttering process. She scaled down her houses and life in California by selling one of her homes and all its contents. She realized she did not need the stuff she wanted to be surrounded by at one time.

Oprah announced to her network viewers, she was downsizing as well. She advertised an auction for her followers interested in acquiring some of her worldly possessions. The benefactor of the auction was her girls school in Africa. Oprah's ability to consume volumes of stuff has enabled her to choose when to acquire and when it is time to let go.

The beneficiaries of her viewing network acquired her closet goods, clothes, household items and artwork she no longer wanted. It was a win-win for her girl's school and viewers wanting a bit of Oprah.

I am not in the same celebrity status as Barbra or Oprah, nor do I want to consume any more than I must. I am not a shopaholic either online, walking the malls, or travelling for souvenir stuff to bring home. I have noticed from my last move, I have boxes of my own stuff that would serve and benefit others.

I had a few autographed books, autographed ticket stubs and athlete autographed postcards and it was time to let go. Gave them to Goodwill and hopefully someone else will monetarily benefit from my tax-deductible donation.

Still Waiting For An Update

While I have not heard from Customer Service on my projected delivery time of my household belongings, I sat among my hand full of boxes and noted how little you can live with and not be destitute.

Customer service does not even answer the phone, after repeated calls, this Saturday morning and voice mail is not connecting.

Is this a tactic to agitate the customer or one where they will get back to you when they have more information? It is starting to feel like I will be sleeping on the floor a few more nights and running out for a salad or burger if nothing arrives.

What I would not give for sleeping in my own bed, or waking up with a cup of coffee to stay in my sweats rather than run out for coffee. It is good having my inspirational books to read in the comfort of my own place rather than going to the library, applying for a library card and sitting there, until it is time to go home to an empty apartment.

What Does Your Stuff Represent?

This move helped me focus on what serves me and how I can be more productive with having less.

Yes, I can be creative and identify multiple purposes for my things. I feel happier and satisfied when my closets are not stuffed with things I do not use or need.

Feeling fulfilled is not about the consumption but rather about 'what I do have has purpose.' How about you?

The Update

Customer service finally returned my call, and said my belongings would arrive in 40 minutes.

My first thought was, "Am I ready?" to move all my stuff into my three rooms. At that point, I wanted to see my stuff, because I knew I had more to downsize as it would fill my tiny apartment.

I said, "Bring it on," and was happy when the truck arrived with my POD. I know the unpacking will be a longer process. I feel compelled to rethink, as I take things out of boxes, do I use it?

If not, does it have a better place in someone else's home?

This process is at each stage of life: when you want to change, you consider the clutter you hold close to heart. You cannot let go of what is holding you back from being the carefree, light spirit you long to be.

*Stuff represents the past, and your ego.
Let go of your past. Your ego is also projecting your future. You can live with less today and Love it Now!*

Your stuff has a purpose. Your ego is reminded of where you have been. Remember, you are in control of letting your ego know you can live with less. Love where you are and release what does not serve you. *Letting go is freeing!*

What are you holding on to?

- ☐ Yesterday's hurts
- ☐ Memorabilia from a grade or High School
- ☐ A Cherished Teddy Bear
- ☐ Furniture not in use
- ☐ College textbooks or notes
- ☐ Jewelry you do not wear
- ☐ Address books from years ago
- ☐ Wedding gifts, do you use today
- ☐ Your child's artwork
- ☐ Photo albums of people you do not remember
- ☐ Fear
- ☐ Lack of self-confidence
- ☐ Doubt
- ☐ _____
- ☐ _____
- ☐ _____
- ☐ _____

Learn more by taking our Assessment Quiz: www.empowermequiz.com

Journal Notes

Do You Have Obstacles, Walls And Boundaries?

As a child, were you the leader or follower going through the corn maze? As the oldest child in our family, I had to be the brave one and be the leader.

Once we started, it was fun to jump over the bales of hay before running through the rows of corn. You screamed or hooted about where you were so others knew your location when they could not see you.

After you exited the maze, you evaluated the path and the challenge of the corn maze. For the adventurous, it meant running through the maze again and faster to give it a 1-10 "maze score," for challenge and fun.

Children love obstacle courses. As an adult, you may feel uninterested or overwhelmed by an unknown path or think it is child's play.

How do you feel going through an obstacle course? There are reality programs today built to challenge your physical and mental strength.

Are you excited about breaking through your own obstacles? Are you proud of your achievement when you overcome your own obstacle?

We establish three barriers for ourselves: obstacles, walls and boundaries. Each has its own purpose. You can remove any of these, depending on your courage or comfort.

Do You Have Obstacles, Walls And Boundaries?

Obstacles

An obstacle does not have to be going through a corn maze.

An obstacle is created any time there is a feeling of being unable to complete a task. An obstacle is a limitation where the goal is to conquer and continue your journey.

Obstacles are self-created barriers you establish because of a perceived or real limitation. The obstacle can be physical or emotional.

You may have created the obstacle to protect yourself from what you feel is harm. The obstacle may be as simple as something in your path blocking you, or a person blocking you from moving forward.

Either way, you are in control of either eliminating the obstacle or telling yourself the obstacle no longer exists.

I faced obstacles earlier in my career when I wanted more flexibility in my work schedule. My commute to work was a minimum of one hour. It was challenging when there were school activities I wanted to attend to support my daughter, while she was growing up.

For me, the tradeoff was I worked half a day to be available to attend morning school functions or being available for after school activities.

Then when I worked in New York City, my commute was 90 minutes each way. My daughter was in middle school and high school and the ability to be home was not as easy as I would have liked.

I decided I would try to be available. There were times I accepted I was not. There was considerable coordination with my husband to be available for my daughter's school activities.

Working from home during those times was not an option. Today there are more options for flexible schedules and working from home or working part time. Many companies have eliminated dedicated work space for employees that do not have to be in the office regularly, thus enabling employees to work from home.

In my time, one of the obstacles was, 'your commitment was measured by how many hours you worked and or in the office.'

You were not considered serious about your job or being a leader unless you worked 50+ hours a week.

Do You Have Obstacles, Walls And Boundaries? 31

Today the standard for working has changed. Many are held to a 24/7 global availability schedule. Employees pick up emails, texts and calls once they leave the office. This around the clock schedule continues until they crash to fall asleep.

There must be balance. It is not healthy to come home, have dinner and then work to pick up emails in the evening so you have a head start for the next day. I worked for a couple of international companies and this was expected.

In today's workplace, we have both real and virtual environments. There are advantages to working from home and have flexibility.

You can feel isolated, at times, and even feel technology challenged if you are not able to connect with other coworkers as needed.

~~~~~~~~

Allowing yourself the ability to overcome your obstacle is breaking down your separation and conquering your own breakthrough.

~~~~~~~~

When you feel isolated, the best question to ask yourself is what resources are available to overcome this limitation? If you cannot do this alone, and would like assistance, ask yourself "Who is available to help me?"

We set our own limitations, especially if we feel the obstacle is the barrier between where we are and where we want to be. When we feel the pain of this limitation, we create a boundary that we must either overcome to feel connected or we will feel stuck and disconnected.

Walls

Walls are structures we build around ourselves.

~~~~~~~~

Just as you cannot walk through a physical wall, the wall is a mental or emotional wall you have built around yourself to protect you from those on the other side or to protect you from something you feel within.

~~~~~~~~

Do You Have Obstacles, Walls And Boundaries?

Walls are the barriers we create as children to protect us from others we felt were going to harm us or to protect our sensitive feelings.

The walls continue to exist into adulthood unless we can manage letting go of the walls. This means being vulnerable and exposing ourselves to others.

The vulnerability may continue today into adulthood until we release the thought no one can hurt us. We are responsible for standing up for ourselves.

It may take time to feel empowered. Each day is a learning process. It is time to learn more about expanding our strength and letting go of isolating ourselves because of our differences.

~~~~~~~~

"For some people, life is the process of knocking through walls to get out. For others, it is the building of walls."

~ Simon van Booy

~~~~~~~~

Boundaries

Boundaries are also established to protect you from others coming too close or exposing your own vulnerability. When you use boundaries in a healthy way, you can release your limitations and establish healthy boundaries.

Boundaries aren't walls, they are speaking up and declaring who we are. Feeling free to speak up is a huge obstacle to overcome.

The past experiences are impacting your ability to be who you are. You may feel guilty about saying no because you haven't been listened to in the past.

I had to overcome this challenge and it is still a challenge. Every day is getting out of my comfort zone and saying "no." It has nothing to do with being defiant, it has to do with speaking up and looking in the mirror to say my voice is powerful. I am empowered to speak up.

When you establish how much you want to share and let others know how you feel, your behavior shows you are fearless, your confidence shows, despite previous vulnerability.

Breaking Through

You create your own personal freedom, when you can break through the walls and obstacles you have created. You will find a new sense of freedom and joy in everything you do.

Do You Have Obstacles, Walls And Boundaries?

The boundaries you created earlier in life to protect you, are no longer needed. As an adult, you can release the walls and feel safe to discover who you are.

The boundaries served at a time you needed them. They now are a healthy barrier your courage and confidence can breakthrough because you are stronger and can speak up for yourself.

The Ball is an example of how the obstacles, walls and boundaries are circling around us. To bust through them, we must break down what keeps us in or we will be overcome.

Quiz:

1. Where have You built obstacles?

   _____

   _____

2. How have the obstacles served You?

   _____

   _____

3. Where are Your walls? How long have You had these walls?

   _____

   _____

4. What are Your healthy boundaries?

   _____

   _____

5. What are You breaking through?

   _____

   _____

Learn more by taking our Assessment Quiz: www.empowermequiz.com

Do You Have Obstacles, Walls And Boundaries?

 *"Every day, I choose to overcome my challenges, be confident, and be the change I want to see in others."*

~ Karen Jones

We can change our thought patterns by being courageous with three actions:

➢ Being aware.

➢ Act to make a change in your life every day.

➢ Repeat a phrase that will encourage your change.

Journal Notes

What Fuels You ?

Have you heard the saying, "Your body knows what it needs, are you listening?"

I have been a foodie, consciously focusing on what I eat and asking myself does it provide energy, or do I feel good after eating.

Every living creature requires nutrition and water to sustain it. Every human body requires the same, and can live on plants and water.

Yes, some bodies also choose their daily dose of meat as well. We can sustain our existence for a short period without food but we will die in 2-3 days without water.

Nutrition

I have always thought of my body as a fine-tuned machine. It is miraculous because it heals itself and knows how to take care of itself.

Dr. Michael Finkelstein, the Slow Medicine Doctor, refers to the human body as a plant. It has living cells, so providing water and nutrition are not optional.

When we ignore the symptoms, and signals the body provides, we have to expect there will be times it cannot perform.

When we allow time for it to heal, by providing the "food," "care," and the "rest" it requires, we are rewarded. It is a living breathing organism. It has a prescribed cycle that sheds and regenerates cells on a regular schedule.

Do you listen and know how to take care of your body? It is a rhetorical question. I have seen women go on diets to starve themselves so they can lose a few pounds. Your body is screaming at you when your choices are not healing or nutritional.

When you starve your body, it is speaking up because it does not know when the next meal will arrive. It requires food to grow new cells.

It is not looking for the maintenance that processed foods provide. It requires wholesome plants with real vitamins, sunshine and water.

The fuel your body requires is the same foods you find in your garden (vegetables and fruits). Your body responds instantaneously with garden fuel.

Brain Food

Do you feed it or starve it?

~~~~~~~~

 *When feeding your body, are you providing the fuel your brain requires to send signals to other body organs.*

~~~~~~~~

When you decide to diet (or fast), you can as long as you feed your brain the constant flow of water, rather than a starvation sprinkling of a little water here and there.

Your brain goes into starvation mode as soon as it realizes there is no consistent flow of water or food (energy). Your brain will conserve its power when you restrict it.

Likewise, it requires the unprocessed fresh garden vegetables rather than out of the box processed foods. Your brain requires WATER, to produce blood to flow through your body to deliver messages to other body parts.

Food Cooperatives

I remember in college, going to a food co-operative to purchase my food staples and veggies.

The food co-operatives offered produce at a significantly reduced price compared to the grocery stores.

Food Co-ops were built on the premise that members who bought shares of the co-op, could receive discounted food purchases. To offset the costs of the co-op, or the members would contribute a few service hours per month.

I remember eating many meals of spinach, alfalfa sprouts, and brewer's yeast in protein shakes, and other whole grains and beans which became a staple in my diet.

I have continued to lead this lifestyle of healthy eating over the last 40 years. Little did I realize then, my health reflects this way of eating with little requirement for vitamins, prescriptions or medical care.

I cannot say it's all in the genes. I have continued eating this way, regardless of the absence of co-ops where I have lived in my adult life.

I have learned my lifestyle has sustained me with providing the energy, weight maintenance, and health benefits that many people are looking for today. You can always start changing your eating habits to improve your health rather than saying it is too late.

There is a science to learn nutrition and how much your body and brain use to operate optimally.

~~~~~~~~

Your personal energy and body performance are dependent on how frequently you consume fruits, vegetables and proteins.

~~~~~~~~

Your body requires fats to perform despite your insistence 'you will become fat from consuming fats.'

When you review the healthy fats such as avocados, olive oil and nut oils versus whole milk, sour cream, fatty cuts of pork, beef, dark chicken meat or poultry skin. The key to a healthy lifestyle is moderation as is everything in life. Moderation is the key.

Inflammation

Today, there is a lot said about disease. When you follow a healthy lifestyle, the goal is to avoid disease, or minimize it.

The question to ask is what causes inflammation in the body. Your lifestyle and what you eat determines what causes your pain and discomfort.

Inflammation is created with irritation, constant rubbing or friction. When you hear the word inflammation, you can imagine a red irritated spot.

That is exactly what is happening inside your body. Your overeating and fat deposits accumulate in your body and are creating friction irritating your organs and interfering with the normal operation of a bodily function.

You had no idea this was happening. It is also caused by inactivity of a body that was made to move, or by blockages or deposits of substances that have caused irritation or overgrowth. The internal organs are overworked to process an abundance of fats and sugars.

When we monitor what we consume and how quickly the body processes the food into energy, we can adjust our consumption to maximize our body's efficiency.

It is best to simply listen to your body when it says, "I am full," and stop eating. It sounds simple but is one of the most challenging areas to minimize disease and reduce inflammation.

We create the inflammation and disease with our own lifestyle. We can overindulge in the pleasure of what is not healthy and nutritious.

We pay the price later. Changing your eating habits is better than waiting for a doctor to restrict them or suffer the consequences of going to an emergency room after inflammation strikes.

What Fuels You ?

What's Your Water IQ?

1. When is your best consumption time?
2. How much undiluted water (not coffee, tea, soda or unsweetened beverages) do you consume?
3. When do you feel most hydrated during the day: Upon waking in the morning, after a meal, after exercising, before bed.
4. Do you pay attention to your level of thirst or hunger during the day? Y or N
5. After caffeinated or alcoholic beverages, do you follow with undiluted water to hydrate your body? Y or N

Learn more by taking our Assessment Quiz: www.empowermequiz.com

Water

We all know it is important to drink water. Do you know why? What is your water requirement and do you consume your share? If not, it shows up in your skin, the flexibility of your joints, even in your bowel movements. It's amazing how a little water can affect so much.

Water in the western world is a commodity that is readily available and often taken for granted. Outside of the western world, clean, safe drinking water is a precious commodity in very short supply.

As Americans, we do take water for granted. While we have the luxury of turning on a faucet and having water readily available, there are places in the U.S. where the water has been contaminated and illness ensues.

Being aware of the water safety in your area is critical. Do you have a supply for at least 3-4 days should your water be affected by contamination or another affliction?

Now for your anatomy lesson.

~~~~~~~~

 *To keep all your organs functioning, your body requires water. Your organs are between 50-65% of water.*

~~~~~~~~

When you are not regularly consuming water, you are forcing your body to squeeze the water out of the foods you eat so it can operate efficiently.

This means when you are drinking beverages such as coffee, tea or soda, your brain is responding to additives of caffeine, sugar or corn syrup and still requires undiluted water.

Your brain is smart and knows when it is on a restricted diet and must restrain its normal functions until more water is consumed.

Water replenishes your blood supply and keeps your internal organs "plump" so they can operate without restriction.

According to Dr. Batmanghelidj (Bat), in his book, *"Your Body's Many Cries for Water,"* the body shows symptoms of dehydration in a number of conditions.

Dr. Bat has "cured" many conditions by prescribing water to his patients.

He treated the following dehydrated conditions:
- Nauseous
- Heartburn
- Migraines
- High Blood Pressure
- Depression
- Abdominal pain

Dehydration shows up in many conditions such as overactive bladder, heartburn, depression and even hunger.

I suffered from migraines, heartburn, and overactive bladder. When I consumed one-half my body weight in ounces of water, it was amazing to feel my symptoms disappeared.

For example, for a weight of 140 pounds, I started drinking 70 ounces a day, and it cleared up my heartburn, overactive bladder and migraines.

My doctor wanted to prescribe medication for overactive bladder and I refused to take the prescription. I was too young and did not want to be on drugs for the rest of my life. When I restricted my coffee consumption, and starting drinking water, I felt amazing.

A simple prescription of water consumption can remedy flushing out the kidneys and bladder of dead cells holding waste products.

Drinking water promotes making more blood, giving the body lighter rather than sluggish movement of blood.

You can experience less headaches, less pain, and premature aging. Water flushes out the kidneys and promotes weight loss. Who does not want to shed a few pounds?

I have many clients tell me they cannot drink too much water, because they must use the restroom frequently.

Well yes, that is the side effect but you are flushing out your kidneys, which is the purpose of drinking the water. Water does not cure everything but give water a chance.

Your health improves because water delivers oxygen throughout your entire body. Your joints are lubricated, and a few more pounds disappear from your body.

Rather than saying how inconvenient it is to drink water or bring it with you over the course of the day, it would be better to feel and look fabulous.

You will see a dramatic change in your disposition, when you are not dehydrated. Your body temperature is warmer so your body perspires and sweats as it runs optimally.

What could be better than 16 ounces of water four times a day.

Where else does your body benefit from water?

I love soaking in the tub with lavender salts. Water is also good for your skin to absorb the water from soaking in a bath. You do not think about the largest organ being your skin and it requires the most water.

When you are in the shower for ten minutes, there is not much opportunity for your entire body to absorb water unless it is soaking in it.

~~~~~~~~~

By soaking in a warm bath, you are reducing the stress your body experiences with stiff muscles and joint pain. The warm water opens your pores to absorb the water, and reduces tension headaches as well as enhances your sleep.

~~~~~~~~~

The steam produced from the warmer water temperature can also open your sinuses and relieve upper respiratory congestion.

There are no side effects from overdoing the water therapy. There are many more by ignoring your body's need for water to replenish itself. So drink up and pamper yourself with water!

Quiz:

1. Do I treat myself to good (nutritious) food?
   - ☐ Daily?
   - ☐ Weekly?
   - ☐ Monthly?
   - ☐ Not at all?

2. Why not, do I deserve it?

   _____

   _____

3. How can I choose what my body and stomach require so they feel better with the foods I eat?

   _____

   _____

4. Do I replenish my body with fresh water?

   _____

   _____

5. Do I soak in a bath or treat myself to the luxury of a bath?

   _____

   _____

6. How do I treat my body? Am I listening to what my body requires?

   _____

   _____

Journal Notes

Do You Have The Energy?

"Call it dance,
call it exercise,
doctors do not care what you do,
as long as the 'Fitbit' counts your daily movement."
~ Karen Jones

Move Your Body

Do you love to move your body? To feel good, you have to move it. You can do this throughout your day or solo behind closed doors. *Just do it!*

The human body was created to perform your daily activities. It has a physical and mental purpose. When you are not moving your body, it feels sluggish.

The blood moving through your veins will slow down to a molasses pace when you decide to sit for hours at a time without giving your body movement and your brain more blood circulation.

~~~~~~~~

I am sure you have heard that sitting is the new "smoking" health hazard! It is because your body was meant to move and be active.

~~~~~~~~

You decide if it is walking, dancing, jumping, gyrating and just plain being in motion. Sitting does not accomplish anything other than keeping your hips stiff and your chair warm.

Have you noticed how difficult or stiff you feel when you have been in one position for a long time?

It is the same reason that patients in hospital beds are moved, to keep their blood flowing and movement of their body to heal.

Do You Have The Energy?

Without this movement, your muscles and internal organs will atrophy. It is a morbid thought but if you are sitting still for long periods of time, this is your wake-up call.

Have you ever been visiting a patient in a nursing home or hospital and they talk about their life regrets? It is an uncomfortable conversation.

Unfortunately, there is no way to step back in time for a "re-take." I know you do not want to have this conversation with family members but it is important to pursue the body movement that you enjoy.

Lack of movement results in accelerated aging and muscle atrophy. Choose One Movement you Love and Stick with it.

Choose the body movement you enjoy. You will be energized by doing what you enjoy. Remember those endorphins you have heard so much about when marathon runners get a high from running 26+ miles.

The endorphins are the hormones released in your nervous system to send feel good messages to your brain when you move your body.

It is the reward for taking action and moving. This is also why you will feel a second "wind" after exercising. Exercising will decrease your feeling of anxiety or frustration due to the hormones released.

You may notice the increase in endorphins released, and feel good about the exercise you just completed.

~~~~~~~~

The movement is generating your own energy. Energy is the force within us that can either inspire or motivate us. A lack of energy is the result of depleted or depressed level of energy.

~~~~~~~~

The easy fix is to "put on some music and dance or move around the room."

It does not matter what you choose to do, as long as you choose. It could be walking, dancing, cycling, swimming, volleyball, softball, or other organized sports, aerobics, Zumba, or any other activities that keep you moving, and yes, even sex.

When you go to an organized exercise class at a health club, gym or dance studio, you will enjoy the movement because the instructor has selected music to energize the activity.

The music is loud to help your brain focus on the activity and get distracted rather than say I do not want to do this and stay on the sidelines.

Teachers are trained how to safely raise your heart rate. The companionship of others in the class makes the group activity more enjoyable. You will feel connected to the group and you will return for another class.

Training Heart Rate Range*				
Age	60 Percent	70 Percent	80 Percent	Maximum
15-19	123-121	144-141	164-161	205-211
20-24	120-118	140-137	160-157	200-196
25-29	117-115	136-134	156-153	195-191
30-34	114-112	133-130	152-149	190-186
35-39	111-109	129-127	148-145	185-181
40-44	108-106	126-123	144-141	180-176
45-49	105-103	122-120	140-137	175-171
50-54	102-100	119-116	136-133	170-166
55-59	99-97	115-113	132-129	165-161
60-64	96-94	112-109	128-125	160-156
65-69	93-91	108-106	124-121	155-151
70-74	90-88	105-102	120-117	150-146
75-79	87-85	101-99	116-113	145-141

Glover, B., Shepard, J., Florence-Glover, S. (1996), *The all new runner's handbook.* Penguin Random House

You will even develop friendships with the women in the class and they are your "dancing diva" friends.

Move your body 3-4 times a week for 20 to 30 minutes of continuous activity where your heart beats above your normal resting heart range, to gain real benefit from your movement.

As the seasons change, the activities you enjoy may change as well. In the winter, you can select from an endless list. Here are a few to choose from dancing, yoga, Pilates, or Zumba class, or outdoor activities such as ice skating, skiing, snowshoeing, rock climbing, or hiking, or other choices you would prefer.

In the summer, you can enjoy walking, running, swimming, hiking or cycling. As the seasons change, you may find you still enjoy outdoor activities versus switching from indoors to outdoors due to inclement weather.

Staying indoors watching sports, or leisure activities where you are predominantly sitting or standing for long periods of time feels limiting.

~~~~~~~~

If you suffer from signs of seasonal deficit disorder or depression, starting an exercise program or class will lessen some of your symptoms.

~~~~~~~~

Please check with your doctor before starting any exercise program, so you are aware of any restrictions your doctor recommends.

Many doctors will encourage movement based on your ability for an activity.

You can see results in a short time, in as little as a couple of classes where you will feel better, and be energized and encouraged to return for more.

The activity also keeps your body warmer. Have you noticed when you are still, you feel cool faster. It is because blood is not flowing to your extremities.

In the military, when soldiers are cold, they keep their hands under their armpits to keep warm.

When you exercise, you will notice you are not getting cold outside as quickly. Blood is flowing and simple movements recirculate your energy.

When you choose an activity, you enjoy, you are more likely to continue it. Rather than saying "I must run or walk every day for 30 minutes."

There are many choices and it is totally up to you to try several things to find something you enjoy.

I have tried many options over the years. I prefer yoga all year round. I have activities in the summer, such as running, walking, playing golf and hiking.

In the winter, I enjoy indoor ballroom dancing, cross country skiing, and ice skating. It takes time to identify what you like. You can choose what you will enjoy and look forward to the social aspect of each sport.

Approximate Calories Burned for a 150-pound person for 30 minutes. *

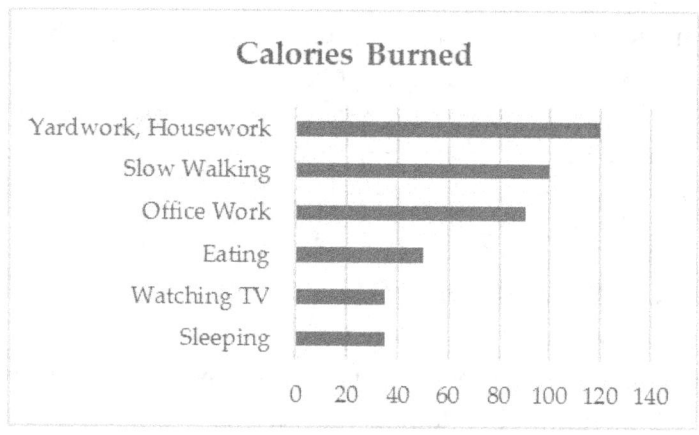

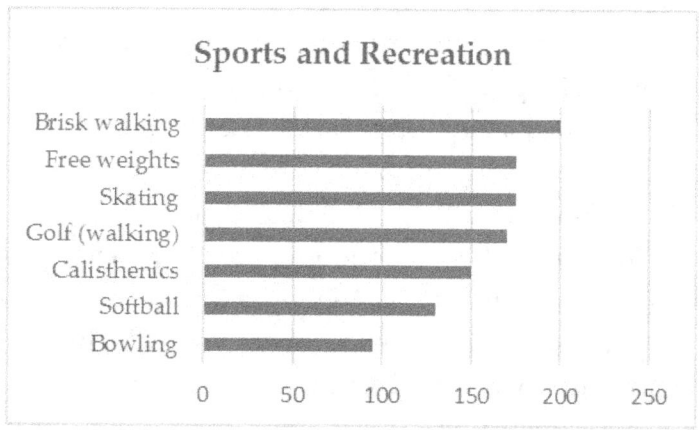

*Glover, B., Shepard, J., Florence-Glover, S. (1996), *The all new runner's handbook*. Penguin Random House. Page 683

For the sports and recreation enthusiast, here are the calories burned in 30 minutes for a 150-pound person.

Notice the Brisk Walking in this chart is 425 calories burned in 30 minutes. The number of calories burned is according to the briskness of the walking.

Sports and Recreation	
Biking	200-300
Aerobic dance	210-270
Tennis (singles)	220-300
Lap swimming	220-300
Soccer	270
Basketball (brisk)	275-375
Slow running (11 min mile)	325
Cross-country skiing	350-500
Brisk walking	425

Movement Quiz

1. What movement feels good to your body?
   _____
   _____

2. What movement do you want to try?
   _____
   _____

3. When can you add movement to your schedule?
   _____
   _____

4. How often do you assess, when it is time to change your routine to feel better?
   _____
   _____

Learn more by taking our Assessment Quiz: www.empowermequiz.com

Journal Notes

What Is Your Sleep 'N Beauty Routine?

Q: Do you know sleep provides the best results for a beauty routine and you get a great night's sleep?

A: Absolutely, sleep is the best wrinkle remover, attitude adjuster and place to dream your best creations.

According to Dr. William Smith, WebMD, the Top 5 Reasons Women Feel Stressed:
1. High Fat Foods
2. Lack of Exercise
3. Difficulties at Work or Home
4. Lack of Personal Joy or Fun
5. Sleep Deprivation

Now is the reason to take getting ready for bed more seriously. Preparing for sleep is not a "crash until you collapse" process. It is knowing that when you take time to prepare for your slumber, you can maximize your rest.

I used to have a full day and always had three more things to do before getting in my bed. Sound familiar? The only one that was short changed on their sleep was me. I sleep through the night, every night, and wake up refreshed and usually just before the alarm goes off. How does that happen?

I love my sleep time. I follow a similar routine in winter and summer. Consistency ensures a peaceful night's sleep.

~~~~~~~~

Your body replenishes and heals while you sleep. When you wake up and are not feeling energetic, ask yourself if you gave your body the best environment and time to rest, replenish and heal while you sleep.

~~~~~~~~

I noticed when I did not get restful sleep or feel energetic in the morning, it was because of two reasons.

One, I was going to bed too late and two, I was collapsing rather than preparing my brain to slow down and adjust for sleep.

We have all suffered from lack of sleep. It contributes to feeling overwhelmed, tired and unable to respond to daily activities.

Lack of sleep also shows up as stress. I knew this all too often when I suffered from the stress and lack of sleep myself.

~~~~~~~~~

Sleep studies have shown that lack of sleep contributes to increased health risks such as heart attack, stroke, type 2 diabetes, and obesity.

~~~~~~~~~

Sleep deprivation also shows up in your slow response time during the day while driving. We have all heard about the car accidents with less than satisfactory results. We do not hear about the dehydrated bodies of sleep and water behind the wheel.

What Is Your Sleep 'N Beauty Routine?

When we sleep well, our beauty shows.

A good night's sleep leads to being more patient, positive and happier during the day knowing you are not running on empty.

Sleeping Check List

Is your sleep routine affected by any of these?

- ❏ Food
- ❏ Caffeine
- ❏ Light or Noise Pollution
- ❏ Addiction to Social Media and TV
- ❏ Cell phone, computer and alarm clock
- ❏ Room Temperature
- ❏ Sleep routine
- ❏ Fresh air
- ❏ Exercise or activity before bed
- ❏ Sleeping aids

Learn more by taking our Assessment Quiz: www.empowermequiz.com

Here are the questions to ask yourself about getting a good night's sleep:

Food

How full is your stomach?

Do you have at least three hours between your meal and going to sleep?

Snacks in the evening also impact your ability to sleep. Your stomach is working at least five hours after a meal to digest your food.

The more you eat, the longer it takes as some foods are slower to digest than others. Your stomach may be screaming "stop" before lying down. Acid reflux is activated when you eat before you go to bed.

~~~~~~~~

Sleep decreases your appetite. If you receive 7-8 hours of sleep, your body is recovering and can rejuvenate itself while you sleep.

~~~~~~~~

Your body is in working mode while you sleep which is why you need more than 3-4 hours to recover from the stress of the day to enable your body to heal itself.

Caffeine

How full is your bladder?

As well as eating, how long ago did you consume an alcoholic beverage or cup of caffeine?

Caffeine stays in the body 8 hours after being consumed. Your afternoon caffeinated coffee or tea will affect your night's sleep with residual caffeine in your system.

Many women tell me that caffeine does not affect their sleep. They do notice they wake up in the middle of the night or when they wake up the next morning, they feel tired rather than rested.

Water and carbonated beverages can also keep you awake, especially if you wake up to empty your bladder.

Light or Noise Pollution

Do you manage light or noise pollution?

Does your bedroom have curtains, drapes or blinds that can be closed to darken the room?

Sometimes, energy efficient lights pollute your room with light.

The darker and quieter the room, the deeper you fall asleep and will stay asleep.

Keeping the light out as well as the noise is an easy step to encourage sleep. It helps if you are not waking up to cars starting or street level noise next to your bedroom window.

Did you know that an open bedroom closet door or the toilet lid open, interferes with your sleep, especially when you can see them from lying in bed?

Seeing your reflection in a mirror from your bed interferes with your sleep.

By ensuring a sound sleep and rest, and paying attention to the room ambiance and setting, you will notice the difference in your peaceful sleep.

TV

Are you addicted to Reality TV?

Take the TV out of your bedroom. If your habit is to watch TV before retiring, STOP. It takes longer for your brain to become unstimulated from the TV.

Move the TV and computer out of the bedroom and stop watching at least one hour prior to going to sleep.

What Is Your Sleep 'N Beauty Routine?

When you cannot go to sleep, plan at least 20 minutes of quiet activity such as reading a book or listening to soft music to give your brain quiet time to relax.

Sleep studies have identified a calming sleep routine affects the quality of your sleep.

Cell Phone and Social Media

We now have a medical condition identified as addiction to Social Media.

Take your cell phone out of the bedroom. If you cannot sleep without it, at least turn the ring to vibrate and move it away so you are not disturbed by the vibration.

Many advertisers send their messages in the early morning hours so you will see them first thing in the morning. The problem is they disturb your sleep.

If you must have your phone on your nightstand, try listening to a phone application that plays quiet music. Ten minutes of soft music or a sleep meditation will put you to sleep.

Alarm Clock or Not

Is your internal clock on automatic?

Does your alarm clock have a lighted face? If it does, turn it away or cover it.

When you wake up in the middle of the night, you do not want to see the time and wonder how long it will take you to fall asleep. This interferes with your restful sleep.

Room Temperature

Are you warm or cold blooded?

Is the temperature in your bedroom 80°+ in summer or 65° or less in winter for sleeping?

A slightly cooler room is more conducive to sleeping because when it is cooler, you can add a blanket to feel more comfortable.

Sleep Routine

Do you have a sleep routine?

Going to bed the same time and waking up the same time creates patterns in your brain for comfort.

It is the same reason you wake up on non-work days as your working schedule. Your brain has built this schedule into its memory bank.

When you are erratic with your wake up and retiring time, you are confusing your brain which is why you are having difficulty falling asleep at night. Your brain does not know if this is a nap or restorative sleep.

Fresh Air / Exercise

What is your fresh air ratio?

Have you noticed spending time outside makes children sleep better? The same will work for you with as little as 15 minutes a day of fresh air. Take a walk. You will see the difference; the walk does not have to be before or after dinner. It can be during the afternoon, lunch time exercise, or a calm activity before bed.

Sleep Aids

Do you take a prescription to help you sleep?

Using a prescription or over the counter product to help you sleep changes the chemistry in your brain.

It can be healthier to take a multivitamin with B vitamins which combats the stress you experience during the day.

Your body consumes the vitamins it needs rather than over the counter products which feel toxic. Your body releases the vitamins it does not need through your urine.

The over the counter remedies stay in your muscles until you can release the toxins.

If all else fails, try a Turmeric Drink.

Following these easy steps provides a consistent message to your brain, for your sleep routine, by slowing down your daily activities.

~~~~~~~~

Savor evening time to enjoy a quiet room with bedding that invites you to sleep.

~~~~~~~~

Your bedroom should be clean and not cluttered. Relaxing means having calm and comfortable surroundings. Lower the room temperature to provide cooler air that helps you sleep.

~~~~~~~~

You can play soft music or read a book, and slow down the last hour of your day to prepare your body and mind for relaxation.

Your sleep will improve along with your mood, level of happiness and energy will rebound!

What Is Your Sleep 'N Beauty Routine?

The recipe for great sleep is to prepare for quiet rest, encourage dreams, feel relaxed and beautiful. You can sleep, dream and feel beautiful.

Turmeric Tea Golden Milk Recipe

Prep time, 2 mins. Cook time, 3 mins. Total time, 5 mins. Serves: 4
*Be advised that the turmeric can stain plastic containers so glass is recommended.
Author: Wellness Mama.com

Ingredients

- 2 cups of milk of choice (almond, pecan, coconut and dairy all work in this recipe)
- 1 teaspoon Turmeric
- ½ teaspoon Cinnamon
- 1 teaspoon raw honey or maple syrup or to taste (optional)
- Pinch of black pepper (increases absorption)
- Tiny piece of fresh, peeled ginger root or ¼ tsp ginger powder
- Pinch of cayenne pepper (optional)
  Instructions
- First, blend all ingredients in a high-speed blender until smooth.
- Then, pour into a small sauce pan and heat for 3-5 minutes over medium heat until hot but not boiling.
- Drink immediately

Journal Notes

Do You Have Hobbies and Schedule Fun?

> From There to Here,
> From Here to There,
> Fun(ny) things are
> Everywhere.
>
> ~Dr. Seuss

What were your childhood hobbies?

Children learn by touching and doing. They are fearless. It is their natural curiosity to discover.

They are explorers into both the real and imaginary world. They are excited about seeing, learning and touching.

Movement is another area children love because of the motion. They love to explore and repeat actions to learn how things work.

You see the joy in their eyes and exclamation on their faces when they are surprised by their own discovery.

They repeat the action over and over with delight while adults are bored or disinterested after a second experience.

~~~~~~~~

Most adults are mesmerized by watching children in their world of play. Maybe a little envious because children are carefree and have no filters.

~~~~~~~~

When was the last time you were fascinated about a new discovery? Can you capture or relive your level of enthusiasm about learning something new?

As we grow older, the level of interest wanes unless we are engaged in satisfying our curiosity to discover new adventures.

Do You Have Hobbies and Schedule Fun?

For some adults, the risk associated with new experiences is overwhelming. Consequently, we minimize the opportunities to explore unless encouraged by friends or family.

This level of learning and discovery is where hobbies were born. As a youngster, there are so many new discoveries to make.

This is especially true when children are identifying what they like to do. It can vary from painting, drawing, writing and other activities with parents or grandparents who shared their hobbies.

You are exposed to many new experiences and can choose which ones you enjoy.

Was it learning about:
- the stars in the sky,
- the world around you,
- an animal that intrigued you,
- wanting a pet, or
- special recipes leading to learning how to cook or
- create something with your hands?

All these experiences were the beginning of the joy of learning and hobbies.

~~~~~~~~~

 *Hobbies ground us. The activity can vary from the visual, mental, or using more of your senses.*

~~~~~~~~~

I enjoyed hobbies because it was time spent with family members or friends and allowed my imagination to soar. For me hobbies became my "go to place," as I could travel to special adventures.

Hobbies provided the exploration to create things using both my visual and tactical skills.

While others love going on a journey, regardless of whether it is real or imaginary, it is all about the joy of the discovery. Where can you go on an adventure to the unknown, be safe, and home for dinner time?

Hobbies can be anything you desire. The goal is to have an activity that takes you to a place where time stands still.

For many, reading is the hobby to travel virtually through the pages of a book to exciting, and exotic places.

For example, in the 1950s, the Nancy Drew series, by Carolyn Keene was about a young girl being a detective and exploring to solve the mystery while on her travels.

I remember the book series provided an opportunity to problem solve, learn how to analyze information and view situations to solve problems.

Do You Have Hobbies and Schedule Fun?

More recently the Harry Potter anthology provided a place for youngsters to enter the world of magical powers, good and evil, and who prevails.

The anthology also revitalized reading in a new generation. Do you remember how many youngsters and adults were brought together because of talking about Harry Potter?

This hobby opened communication between generations and opened doors to new and exciting computer games, creative spaces, reading groups and libraries filled because of the Harry Potter craze.

How many engage in hobbies as an adult?

Hobbies encourage you to explore, create and discover what makes you feel happy? When you think of a hobby, how do you feel?

Results of a recent survey, *Ask Your Target Market*:
- 24% said they have one hobby and practice or participate it regularly
- 56% said they have multiple hobbies
- 74% felt hobbies are important
- 66% said they were time consuming and would like to spend more time on hobbies.
- 20% of the surveyed group does not have a hobby.

Next Phase

As we progress in continuing our education and in our careers, there are times when the hobbies we enjoyed earlier in our lives are sidelined for a variety of reasons.

Whether you do not have the equipment, the time or lost interest in the activity, when you pursue a hobby, you re-energize the inner child.

Connecting with the hobbies from earlier in your life or finding new hobbies are the outlet to enjoy time outside work. Hobbies also allow you to connect with family members when it is a common interest you share.

Entrepreneurs say their hobby has evolved into their business. Women say your passion is the hobby that develops into your career.

For those that pursue their hobbies and can make a living monetizing their hobby, it is passionate work.

Hobbies are an outlet. Regardless if you do not think you have interest or time for them, they provide a real-time opportunity to escape from reality to explore what makes you happy.

It provides a comfort zone like the place it provided as a child. As an adult, the comfort zone a hobby provides is like "hobby healing" with an energizing sense of adventure, curiosity, and creativity that enables you to soothe the heart and mind.

When asked, "What is your hobby?" it does not matter if it provides the healing you seek when you revert to the activity.

Research has identified those with hobbies are happier people.

As you age and may have more time alone, the hobby provides comfort. Hobby healing also lessens the feelings of depression or mental fatigue, if you do not have family or friends nearby.

My favorite hobbies are sewing and making quilts. I have even made gifts that I sell on Etsy. I enjoy making jewelry and collecting items for my dollhouse.

I enjoy playing golf, especially when I travel. Playing golf on courses that were designed by the Golf Masters is exciting. I enjoy travelling and have my bucket list of places I still would like to visit.

I also enjoy ballroom dancing and big band and jazz music. All my hobbies provide happiness and joy that carries into other areas of my life.

They provide creativity when I'm writing. They provide creativity to imagine new quilting projects. When I am in a new area, I go exploring. I look for new discoveries, adventures and learn about the culture. This sense of curiosity is a bug that grows and I have learned so much from my sense of adventure.

There are activities you may have enjoyed as a child, that developed into a skill to earn a living.

It varies from:
- painting,
- singing,
- dancing,
- playing a musical instrument,
- playing sports,
- being artistic,
- cooking,
- collecting something such as dolls, stamps or a collection you enjoy.

The world of hobbies can equally be personal to you.

Do You Have Hobbies and Schedule Fun?

Hobbies are FUN!

1. Which of your childhood hobbies do you still enjoy today?

❏ Puzzles	❏ Theatre (Singing, Acting)
❏ Board Games	❏ Sports
❏ Stamp/Coin Collecting	❏ Pets (dogs, cats, fish, reptiles)
❏ Dolls or Collecting Dolls	❏ Woodworking / Furniture
❏ Baking or Cooking	❏ Reading
❏ Gardening	❏ Travel
❏ Crafts / Sewing	❏ Dancing
❏ Building Blocks	❏ _____
❏ Painting / Drawing	❏ _____

2. If you do not have any hobbies, why not?

   _____

   _____

3. What is stopping you?

   _____

   _____

Learn more by taking our Assessment Quiz: www.empowermequiz.com

Do you Schedule FUN?

Do you have fun?
- ❑ Daily?
- ❑ Weekly?
- ❑ Or want more fun in your life?

When you feel the stress of life, or you are not fulfilled as you once were in your career, take a time out.

The time to escape to ask yourself what provides the fun to feel satisfied. Fun is not a temporary feeling.

~~~~~~~~

 *Fun is identifying the things you enjoy doing that brings happiness. When you are happy, you are content. Less will upset you when you feel content.*

~~~~~~~~

Do You Have Hobbies and Schedule Fun?

When you are lacking something in your life, where is the FUN that is missing?

It may be as simple as:
- ➢ treating yourself to a bouquet of flowers,
- ➢ walking through a flower shop,
- ➢ going to the movies,
- ➢ bowling,
- ➢ taking photographs in a garden or in a museum,
- ➢ going to your favorite coffee shop,
- ➢ writing in your journal about a special place you enjoy visiting,
- ➢ taking a walk in a special place where you enjoy the surroundings.

Is it missing the connections with girlfriends? Quality time with your spouse or special companion? Talking on the telephone with a friend you have not heard from in a long time? Reconnect with your sense of FUN? It is different for everyone.

Make sure you schedule FUN time. Your time is valuable and enjoying FUN activities are treasured when they are missed. On your calendar, list three times a week that you are doing a fun activity. If three does not work for you, at least, find one to start your weekly Fun activity.

What will you schedule for FUN next week?

Journal Notes

What About Your Spirituality Practice?

"Mindfulness is about creating your own internal magic. Meditation is one of the ways to quiet your mind."

~ Karen Jones

When you say spirituality, what does that mean? Many people admit they are not religious.

You can be religious, and not be spiritual and vice versa.

Spirituality is the umbrella of how we feel connected to everything in our lives. Being connected to People is covered in the chapter on Relationships and Connections.

I am referring to the energy and feeling within. We are all energetic energy. Your energy can be labelled either active energy or quiet, calm energy.

The active energy can be felt when we feel energized and charged with enthusiasm. The calm energy is when we can transform the active, happy energy with a technique to feel calm and peaceful inside.

Being mindful is having an inner calm. For some people, there is too much noise going on in their head and they do not feel the ability to be calm or peaceful.

The noise or chatter in their head can be calmed by sitting quietly and letting go of the noise. This practice is not an easy one and can be learned to provide tranquility within.

There is Room to Be Spiritual, even when you hear Drama and Chatter.

Here Is The Drama

We have heard the expression, "I want it NOW."

Saying, "I want it now," sounds like a temper tantrum. It is easy to identify what you do not want.

We are programmed, from infancy, to say what we do not want. It is ironic how "No" is learned faster than "Yes."

Even toddlers realize they have more power being defiant with "No," and they demonstrate their cue more frequently.

The toddler's motor skills are not developed to say, "Mommy, I would like something else." The word, "No," is repeated until they get the attention they want, or a better choice is offered.

Do you ask for what you want? Sounds easy but in many instances, I have found it is easier to eliminate the choices I do not want, so I can identify what I do want.

We should boldly say "I want this!"

I grew up in a household where childhood assertiveness was not encouraged. It was more important to be content with what you were given. It became equally important for me to identify what I desired and how to create what I wanted.

When we create, it takes more energy, more thought, and time to identify exactly what we desire. Our creation is not materialized until we hit our eureka moment!

As adults, we may need a time out occasionally rather than having a temper tantrum. Have you been in a conversation with a family member and you feel stress increasing in your conversation?

Your frustration is not caused by the other person. It is your reaction that surfaces in response to this situation. An adult time out is two minutes.

When you have released the stress, you can come back to the conversation after you are aware of your response.

I found the best way to handle this is to excuse yourself from the exchange, while you feel the agitation or frustration, and if that is not possible, to start taking a few deep breaths.

What About Your Spirituality Practice?

When you are able to go to another place to diffuse what you are feeling, your ego is showing up in the stress, frustration or agitation and it wants to be in control.

Today as an adult, ask for what you want. Can you articulate what you desire, and visualize to create it?

Regardless whether it is a new job, a purchase, or a relationship that does not exist right now, creation takes time. Why not take the time to create the vision of what you want?

Yes, it takes planning, patience and persistence. Your personal programming will bring you what you are manifesting.

Are you ready to start creating what you really desire in your life? When we step out of 'No," and into "Yes," we create. Our creation arrives in its exquisite form miraculously.

Here Is How To Calm The Drama With A Time Out

Just breathe, Take Several Deep Breaths:

Taking deep breaths allows the oxygen to enter your lungs and the few seconds of pause is what your body requires to diffuse a situation.

Take two or three deep breathes to release the stress you feel in your body.

If that does not work, stand up, close your eyes, and start again.

Take five deep breathes-- slowly and deeply, hold the breath for a couple of seconds before letting go.

To release the stress, let go of everything else on your mind to focus on these few breathes.

Then continue breathing for a few minutes, each time hold your breath 2-3 seconds until you release the stress.

When you feel the relaxed feeling, you have achieved the benefit of a Time Out. This is mindfulness.

~~~~~~~~

"When we have peace in our hearts and minds, we draw peace into our lives."

~ Iyanla Vanzant

~~~~~~~~

Stress Is The Mindful Chatter

Living in a state of stress takes a toll on your body. Stress shows up in ways you may not connect, such as anxiety, frustration, anger, diet cravings, disease, body aches, pain and depression.

When you minimize your stress or factors causing stress, you will feel energized and happier.

The weight of the stress in your muscles is toxic. Your shoulders and back will physically lift as the stress is released in your body.

Take An Outdoor Break

If you frequently feel spending time outside or with your pet helps you release stress, take advantage of walking your dog.

While your pet enjoys the time, checking the neighborhood, getting the exercise, you too will benefit from the bonding and change of scenery. Yes, even on the days when the weather is not perfect, you benefit from the fresh air.

Spending time outdoors, sitting in the sunshine, or the rain, or playing with your pet dissolves stress. Your pet recognizes the change in your attitude as well.

Pets are quite perceptive in their response to receiving your love as well as giving their attention to you when you require it.

Meditation Is Your Inner Experience

Do you meditate?

Meditation is a relaxation technique where you establish a process to calm your brain to relax from all the noise you experience throughout the day.

~~~~~~~~

 *When you create this relaxation practice you are reframing the way you think and creating a calm so you feel peaceful when there is noise or distractions.*

~~~~~~~~

There are many forms of meditation, including yoga. The purpose of meditation is to sit quietly to release the thoughts that are active in your mind.

By learning the technique of slowing active thoughts, that have impulsive responses, you are able to deflect the spontaneous reactions that create stress.

By releasing the thoughts, you are managing a mindset of peace, calm and relaxation.

Vision Or Mantra

Meditation also consists of creating a soothing picture in your mind. The vision you see is one that brings joy.

The place you can retreat to when you need a respite. This Joy can be sitting on a park bench, walking at the beach, sitting in a tree (the one you loved as a child), being in lush forest, in a canoe on a lake, or whatever feels peaceful and soothing to you.

~~~~~~~~

 *You can say a mantra which is a few words you repeat to bring you to the calm peaceful place, such as "I am a calm person," or "I am releasing all distractions to be at peace."*

~~~~~~~~

Repeating the mantra, silently for a few minutes and continue to do so when new thoughts come to mind, breaks the pattern in your brain to stop and listen to the messages you hear.

By repeating this practice when you feel stress, you are controlling your thoughts. You are sending the message to your conscious mind that you are not listening to random thoughts. You will return to this quiet place and enjoy a feeling of calm and relaxation regularly.

How long does meditation last? When you start the process, it can be for as little as 5 or 10 minutes.

You can increase the time as you feel comfortable. Meditation is a routine to feel peaceful.

It does not happen once and then you can stop. This is a practice you can continue a few times a week or ultimately every day.

Establish a routine for meditation. When would you like this feeling, when you wake up in the morning or before you go to bed. You can take as little as 10 minutes during lunch or practice several times a day, whenever you feel the stress of the day.

Clarity And Focus

Like the vision that brings you peace and calm, meditation brings you clarity and focus. It allows you to calm the noise around you and creates a space where your thoughts are focused on what is important.

You do not hear the noise stirring because you can turn it off.

Each of these steps can work independently on their own or collectively creating a place of calm.

What Is Your Mindful Practice?

1. Do you regularly have a quiet practice?
   _____
   _____

2. How do you create your own inner calm?
   _____
   _____

3. Have you noticed the difference when you skip your practice?
   _____
   _____

4. What is your goal in each session?
   _____
   _____

   - ❏ To feel quiet?
   - ❏ Release stress?
   - ❏ Reprogram your brain?
   - ❏ Love yourself more?

Learn more by taking our Assessment Quiz: www.empowermequiz.com

Journal Notes

Are You Satisfied With Your Relationships?

Remember the phrase: "You can't live with them and you can't live without them?"

~ Anonymous

You are not alone in this lifetime. You are connected to others.

How do you feel about your relationships and connections?

- ☐ Longing to feel connected?
- ☐ Feel there's too much drama?
- ☐ Interact more on your phone than in person?
- ☐ Feel relationships are too much work?
- ☐ Only get hurt?
- ☐ Aren't strong enough for the heartache?
- ☐ Push people away with your boundaries?
- ☐ Other reasons?

What does it take to hold your attention?

Somedays it feels like I have Attention Deficit Disorder (ADD) because there are so many things that distract my attention.

~~~~~~~~

I make a conscious effort to focus on what is important. There is information overload and it is easy to be distracted.

~~~~~~~~

I have found Social Media, TV and my cell phone are frequent places I can lose focus.

Are You Satisfied With Your Relationships?

If you have a short attention span, your symptoms can be magnified as well. You can be distracted easily with the shiny objects attracting your attention rather than focus on what is important.

Has this happened to you?

Have you gone to Starbucks and while waiting in line, you notice how distracted people are for a few minutes by their cell phones?

It only takes a few minutes to focus on your phone before it is time to give your order. Then, while you are waiting for the barista to make your coffee, you are back on your phone.

What is so important that you cannot take 10 minutes away from your phone to chat with the person next to you in line?

We all want to feel connected. We do not want to miss that important phone call, text or email but at what expense?

Do you feel better connected or worn out because of ensuring you have not missed any connections?

Do you leave work to pick up your text or email messages until bedtime and then leave the phone on your night stand for a good night's sleep? Really, who is calling at 3 a.m.?

It is one thing to be connected 24/7, and it is another to be able to walk away and have a conversation with a child that wants your attention or a pet, let alone your partner. The phone, text and emails will be there when you are in control of how to connect with others.

There's A Price To Pay For Immediate Connectivity

Would you love to return to the days where every day is carefree, fun and creative?

We all carry the weight of the world on our shoulders. I am referring to taking time out of your day to reconnect with others. Yes, I know, everyone wants your attention.

Can you let go of the burden of the extra workload or stop picking up emails to enjoy your creative, carefree self?

It is a shift from staying in worry and pain. Just let go, because the shift allows more creativity, joy, happiness, money, and even more importantly, what you desire in your life.

"Connection is the energy that is created between people when they feel seen, heard, and valued." ~ Brene' Brown

Communication

"Some people love talking in the spotlight.
While others love to listen.
Some enjoy the drama.
While others enjoy the banter."
~Karen Jones

There are two ways to connect with others, either by talking or touching.

Mind reading is not an option; it is the least effective. There are many opportunities for missed interpretation.

Communication is the key to connecting with others. You have two options, verbal and nonverbal.

We all know that nonverbal communication (body language) speaks louder than your words.

There is a lot to learn about body language and attitude. Psychology studies reveal body language represents more than one half of your message while verbal communication is less than 10%.

Verbal is more effective, although you can also send mixed verbal messages. Mastering verbal communication takes time. Its rewards are long lasting.

~~~~~~~~

 *Despite all the current technological and medical advances, there is no replacement for sitting next to someone and speaking to them.*

~~~~~~~~

Even when you are unhappy with someone, and choose to confront them, and deliver your message, they will honor you for your honesty.

They may not be happy with your message and when you start the dialogue of a conversation, it is opening the door for two-way communication.

It is far less effective to wait and delay the conversation while you are feeling frustrated.

Starting the conversation in a time of frustration does deliver a message which may not reflect your original intention.

Be open and honest and state your intention to learn about the other person in the conversation.

Socializing

When you feel, you are not able to start a conversation, remember:

People love to talk about themselves,

All you have to do is say "hello" and ask a question.

It is easy:
- What did you enjoy about your day today, yesterday or over the weekend?
- What is your favorite sports team?
- What type of food do you enjoy?
- Tell me about your favorite restaurant? Or favorite meal?
- Where is your favorite vacation spot?
- Tell me about your last trip there?
- What type of music do you like?
- Tell me about your family? Your children? Your hobbies?

Wouldn't you love to talk about what you enjoy, it is easier than you think.

The only way the conversation can be short is when the other person responds with "I dunno."

You can prompt for more information or ask another question. When you ask questions that require more than a yes or no, you will engage the other person in a conversation.

~~~~~~~~

 *The most important thing to remember, they may feel the same way as you. When you start the conversation, you will break the ice and have accomplished your goal.*

~~~~~~~~

I did not say it was easy but it is breaking the silence and making a connection.

No one can read your mind and thankfully that's a good thing. There are many situations, where lack of mind reading is a blessing.

The same holds true for communication with family members, and friends.

Similarly, conversations with people you want to get to know romantically, start with an intention to be open and authentic.

Breaking the Ice

Are you aware of how to start the conversation?

Question: When you meet someone you want to interact with, how do you want to respond?

- ➤ He's attracted to you by how he sees you (he's visual).
- ➤ You may not like him, but respect him, if he approached you and you do not want to continue the conversation, excuse yourself.

Are You Satisfied With Your Relationships?

- Do not pay more attention to your phone than the conversation.
- Have a sense of humor.
- You will get his attention if you are confident and open.
- You can hold the conversation.
- You do not talk about yourself.
- You listen.

Communication Tips

Extroverts:
- Love to talk, and love to hear themselves talk.
- They speak first before thinking what they will say.
- They are verbalizing their thoughts aloud.
- Extroverts conclude introverts are not listening.

Introverts:
- Gather their thoughts and then speak.
- A conversation is quiet with an introvert, they are processing the conversation before they speak.
- They are more thoughtful.
- Introverts speak slowly and extroverts interrupt them.

Learn more by taking our Assessment Quiz:
www.empowermequiz.com

Journal Notes

Have You Arrived At Joy?

"I want you to forget everything you have learned in your whole life.

This is the beginning of a new understanding, a new dream.

The dream you are living is your creation."

~ Don Miguel Ruiz,
The Four Agreements

Your new place of being is Joy.

When you embrace your life, and live in the moment, it is your place of "being."

It is the calm and inner peace you experience when you are in meditation. It is an expansive place.

Taking a deep breath, you feel your lungs expand. You are allowing space for new breath to enter your life. It is where you feel alive and you are recharged from within.

~~~~~~~~

When your life is ever changing and constantly in motion, you will love all the new places of discovery. There is a change in your behavior, in your attitude, in your opinion and how you approach each day.

~~~~~~~~

You have an energy that feels like you have taken a "happy" (endorphins) pill. It is you on steroids and you have found what some women say, "is being comfortable in their skin."

Take that to a higher level, when you, "Feel perfect in the right place, at the right time, and that is Now."

When you choose to be open, and vulnerable, and receptive to making new choices, your world becomes a new and exciting place.

Rather than choices that came in the past with doubt and frustration. Now choices come with excitement, electricity and joy because a new part of you is blossoming.

You feel a new confidence. You can express what you love about your life.

You embrace your life because it feels like you have finally arrived. You are ready for the party and celebration of who you are. This is Joy.

Adventure

The journey is being able to identify where you want to go, with whom and for how long.

When was the last time you went on an adventure? Was your location ideal?

Were your activities planned and did they provide the outlet you were looking for?

The Joy of Adventure is the place we choose to experience life. It is where we go for a momentary rendezvous or hours to experience.

The adventure is to learn, dream or put our feet on the ground and explore. It can be a brand-new place or explore our next horizon.

Adventure is exciting when we allow ourselves to discover what is beyond our reach. Enjoy life's adventure and all it offers you.

 *"Think positive and positive things will happen."*
- *Buddha*

Positivity

What is this new attitude?

It is called positivity.

You have made new friends. They have similar attitudes of openness and possibility. You can see how your attitude of appreciating what you have and can see how it affects the joy in your life.

The relationships of the past and emotional attachment to things that are not working for you, can be released because they do not serve you. Letting go of the past does not affect you.

Your positivity carries you to a higher place. To Love.

Love

Love is Joy. Joy is Bliss.

Love is the joyous melody your heart plays when it is in a blissful state. How do you arrive at bliss?

You listen to the voice within your heart that rejoices when you can love others and yourself.

 *There is too much time spent on regret. We are granted a finite number of days in this life. Why not live them joyfully each day!*

Bliss is the state rejoicing in every area of your life. There is no second guessing your actions. You are present, focusing on the moment now, releasing the past which you cannot change.

The only important place to be is exactly "here and NOW and Love it!"

You have the most important relationship with yourself living in Joy and Bliss.

Gratitude

How many times a day do you say, "Thank You?"

It does not mean you are ungrateful if you do not say thank you. It means you are aware of how much more you bring into your awesome life when you express gratitude.

Thank You

- For acknowledging there are great things in your life.
- For having family and friends to love.
- For your heart that is beating.
- For having clean air to breathe.
- For prayer and having gratitude.
- For speaking up for who you are.
- For having the choice to do whatever you want, whenever you want, with whom you want.

Thank You for all your blessings, those you are aware of and even those you are not.

About the Author

Karen Jones, is the Founder/ CEO of KScope Focus, after discovering and experiencing there is a better life to live. She created a collaborative approach in coaching and training programs to enable numerous professionals to overcome their resistance to change.

She experienced life's rollercoaster ride when her marriage of 22 years ended when her husband unexpectedly left her.

Then two years later, she became an empty nester, when their daughter went off to college.

She felt feelings of abandonment and not in control and five years later, she was part of a corporate downsizing.

Karen looks at change as the shake up to letting go of the past, embracing the next adventure, and enjoying the journey.

As a result, she started KScopeFocus to support other professionals experiencing lack of fulfillment and frustration in their career, and ready to take the leap to start something new. She overcame her own obstacles but wished there had been a guide to make it easier.

She enjoyed her work in three global companies where helping others embrace change was empowering.

Her career guided managers and executives through the relocation process, and assimilated expatriates in bi-cultural work environments resulting in shorter transition time.

She was energized by the corporate culture, organizational change and employee engagement syngergies.

She's studied with Brendon Burchard, John Assaraf, Darren Hardy, John Gray, Andy Lothian, Loral Langemeier and Jane Deuber.

She holds a Master's degree in Organization Management and Human Resources Development from Manhattanville College.

She is a Certified Health Coach with AADP (American Association of Drugless Practitioners).

She currently lives in the beautiful Southwestern part of the United States.

Her website is www.kscopefocus.com.

Gratitude for Support on My Journey

This book would not be possible without expressing gratitude to those who have supported me on my journey. Your timely support guided me to discover what is important and made this book possible.

Thank you to Penny Cohen who provided inspiration to write and learn from the life lessons the Universe sent me. This project provided my path to help others. Your ongoing supporting in my transition years was instrumental on my journey to find love and joy again.

Thank you to the leaders I have worked with who pushed me out of my comfort zone. A particular thanks to Bill Weld, Pat Dinley, Pat Wheeler, Jamie Guerrero, Bill Curran, Kevin Doran, Don Welsko, Jamie Benton, Larry Glass, Clayton Broemsen, Ian Dewar and John Kessinger. There are many more who also pushed me; I am grateful for your nudge.

Thank you to Lynn Powell for support, after I left my corporate career. Thank you for listening, when I needed to talk through those challenging times.

Thank you to Carol Farabee, for editing and publishing my work, which felt heavy on the manuscript pages. The clouds were edited and shaped into puffs that matter on the page. Your edits now contribute to this lovely landscape.

Thank you to Belinda Rosenblum and David Newman for their coaching. Gratitude to David for pushing me to write each chapter with love and compassion, so other women, on their journey of transformation, can discover the next chapter to their inner self.

Thank you to Becky Gorton, Donna Sparaco and Karen Joseph. Your connection on my Arizona stop provided valuable pivoting to what was next.

Thank you to Debbye Cannon. Your friendship and introduction to Strongbrook's Limitless, helped me see, that the move to Utah was the next opened path from the Universe.

Finally, thank you to my parents for pushing me to stretch for what I desire. To my daughter, son-in-law and granddaughter who are the inspiration and motivation to provide more love in my life.

To friends and business connections I have made on my path and gratitude to the Universe for the perfect timing on this journey.

Living The Joyful Life You Design

www.ingramcontent.com/pod-product-compliance
Lightning Source LLC
Chambersburg PA
CBHW071601220526
45469CB00003B/1085